W9-AKC-761

ISBN 0-935493-09-3
Gifted, Precocious, or Just Plain Smart
ᶜCopyright 1987, by Priscilla L. Vail.
Printed in the United States of America.
All rights reserved. No part of this book
may be used or reproduced in any manner
whatsoever without written permission
except in the case of brief quotations
embodied in critical articles and reviews.
For information address Programs for
Education, Inc., Rosemont, NJ 08556.

Gifted, Precocious, or Just Plain Smart

A Story for Puzzled Parents

Written by
Priscilla L. Vail

Illustrated by
Frank Weiss

Published by
Programs for Education, Inc.
Rosemont, NJ

PROLOGUE

As each child is a gift, so each child comes with distinguishing gifts. For some, the balance makes for a tranquil passage through life. For others, the balance produces frustrations, dreams, and energies which resemble the tides of the sea in their power and relentlessness. Giftedness brings its own particular set of pleasures and perils.

Gifted children have intense emotional and social needs that are frequently sacrificed to intellectual or academic concerns, particularly when educators get into the act. Being a teacher myself, I feel a license to criticize my own profession which I might deny to an outsider.

One worry is that as giftedness nudges other special educational needs aside in the popular and professional press, two things are happening. The first is a denigrating of the needs of gifted children. This springs from a philosophical discomfort with the idea of favoritism for an endowed elite. We prize equality so highly that superlative performance is often suspect. Paradoxically this coexists with ready applause for superheroes in sports, moneymaking, and daredeviling. The idea of singling out one element of the population for special support is mistrusted unless the element is below the average. It is idealistically comfortable to help the underdog. Topdog is supposed to take care of himself.

The second cause for my concern is the limelight recently thrown on a group of children labeled "the gifted and talented." Suddenly these children are the focus of a great deal of governmental and professional attention. Their lives will be microscopically examined, they will be the objects of studies, and the recipients of hot, new, educational materials. This may be wonderful, or it may not. It all depends on whether the live child is found in the program or sacrificed to it.

As a teacher and a parent I want to share what insights I have with others who are concerned with children: educators, parents, physicians, those who plan community projects, and enlightened caretakers who want to protect and support gifted children so they may grow into whole people.

Prologue reproduced by kind permission of Walker and Company, New York.

The Story of
Evan-Everything

"**E**van-Everything."
The kids in school sometimes call me that. I like knowing about lots of different things, and it's usually easy for me to remember them.

Sometimes I learn by listening. I know a lot about electricity and gears from hearing my dad and his friends talking, and I've learned how to make electric circuits. My mom is a dietician so I know some things about bodies and nutrition from listening to her. I hear things on TV too, and I know lots of stories from the records and cassettes from the library. If I listen to a song, even just once, I can sing it back and sometimes even play it.

I learn from looking around, too. There are patterns everywhere if you take time to see them. You can find lots of patterns on buildings. How many different shapes; squares, rectangles, arches? How many windows, how many rows? Sometimes shapes look good because they balance each other. That's called symmetry. (I learned that word from TV.) Sometimes designs look better when they don't balance. And it isn't just the things you *see;* some music balances and some doesn't.

People balance too, at least on the outside. Two arms, two legs, two eyes, two ears. Even though you've only got one nose, it has two holes, and your mouth has two lips. But what about when you feel a special way? My feelings don't always match up. How about ideas? Are they supposed to come in pairs? And where do they come from anyway?

*S*ometimes when somebody starts to explain something to me I already understand about it, even new stuff. My mom and dad say I'm like the circuits I build; all the wires are laid down, all I need is a couple of words to be a switch and my light goes on. The kids in school started calling me "Evan-Everything" because they said I knew so much. At first I liked it and I told my parents. They smiled, but they looked worried too.

I liked nursery school and kindergarten. I was allowed to play with blocks, and paint, and sing. They let us play with the wagons, and pretend to be wild animals, and I had fun with the other kids. The teacher read to us every day, and sometimes we played games about the story. I knew how to read by myself, but I didn't tell anybody because I liked sitting in the circle listening to the teacher read. At home I looked at library books or my own books, and I had time to play.

*W*hen I started first grade everybody told me I would discover new things. I kept on waiting; I sat in my desk chair and waited. The teacher gave us workbooks and worksheets. At first I liked the workbooks. I pretended I was my dad sitting at his desk. After workbook time, we were supposed to line up for what the teacher called "corrections." I don't mind fixing mistakes, but some of those workbook pages were wrong.

*O*ne page had four pictures; a dog, a taxi, some vegetables, and a cat. We were supposed to circle the picture that started with the c sound. First I circled two pictures, then I circled all of them. Here's why. *Cat* was obvious, but *canine* is another word for dog so I circled that too. Then I looked at taxi and remembered that a taxi is also called a *cab,* and then I looked at the vegetables and they looked like salad. Well, *carrots* and *cucumbers* go in salad so then I had a way to make all four pictures match. I was excited to show my teacher but she marked my page wrong. When I told her what I had figured out she wasn't excited at all. She told me not to be obstinate. I don't know what that means yet, but it doesn't sound very friendly.

That's how school is lots of the time. Math is mostly work sheets, and if you know how to do one kind of problem you just get more. Yesterday I got 50 additions and 50 subtractions. Most of the other kids got 25, except Henry. He got ten because he's so slow.

*W*hen I got through, the other kids were still working so I figured out something new. I went back and marked each *plus* problem with a Y for Yes if you could also do it as a *minus*.

$$\begin{array}{r} 4 \\ +\,3 \\ \hline \end{array}$$ got a Y,

$$\begin{array}{r} 2 \\ +\,5 \\ \hline \end{array}$$ didn't.

Then I worked all the *minus* problems as *plusses* and wrote the extra answer beside the real one. Here's one that struck me as funny.

$$\begin{array}{cc} 9 & 9 \\ \underline{-7} & \underline{+7} \\ 2 & 16 \end{array}$$

The difference between 16 and 2 is 14, and 14 is two times 7, and 7 is in each problem!

I showed my teacher what I had done but she said "We don't have time for this kind of thing." Then one kid said I was a show-off, and then they started saying "Evan-Everything" to me. I didn't like it. I didn't want to feel ashamed of what was exciting.

After that, I just did my work sheets and my workbooks, and I tried to stay interested in the stories in the reading book, but school made me feel sad. Some days the other kids were nice to me at recess and lunch, but sometimes they acted like I wasn't even there, or they yelled "Evan-Everything" and there wasn't anything I could say back.

I used to like my name. My mom had a girl cousin named Evan and my dad had a boy cousin named Evan. Both the Evans are good at math and art, and they are lots of fun. When we have big family parties all of us Evans sit together. But my name doesn't sound good when the other kids say it that way.

I stopped doing things at home after school. It was already the middle of the afternoon when I got there, too late to start up anything interesting. Besides I didn't really feel like doing anything except sitting around waiting.

*O*ne night I was up in my room but I could hear my parents talking. My mom said "Do you suppose Evan is gifted?" My dad said "I don't know how you tell, and maybe I don't want to find out. I don't know if I want my kid sent to some special program."

He said "I know the kid is precocious, but maybe that'll just wear off." My mom said "But maybe really smart kids need a whole different education."

I got scared. Maybe there's something the matter with me. What's gifted? What did Dad mean about sending me to a special program? Were they going to send me away? What's precocious? I've never even heard the sound of that word... it sounds like something with spikes on it. And about being smart, I used to feel smart till I started real school. Now I feel like my ideas are having a fight with my teachers.

I only got a 75 on my worksheet today. Does that mean I'm not smart anymore? Is that why they're thinking about sending me away? Sending me away! I got so scared I just started crying out loud. I ran into the room where they were talking and said "Don't send me away!"

They didn't know what I was talking about, and when I tried to explain it came out all jerky because I was crying so hard. First they told me not to be silly, and then when they saw I was really scared, they promised never to send me away. They said they were trying to find out how I could get more fun out of school, the way I used to. They said they were worried about how quiet I had gotten, and how I seemed sad. I felt safe when they said that word. I knew they understood.

The next morning they asked me if I wanted to take piano lessons. I said it would depend on what the teacher would make me do. In school, my teacher makes me do reading exercises even though I already know how to read. I can already play the piano some. I don't want the same thing to happen.

*T*hat same day, my mom called the school to see if they have any programs for gifted children, and how they decide who is eligible. She found out they have a program for middle schoolers with an IQ above a certain number. But middle school is a couple of years away.

So Mom called a friend of our family's named Mrs. Anderson. She's been a teacher and a school principal for more than thirty years. She also has something called a doctorate, but she's not the kind of doctor who gives shots. Mom asked Mrs. Anderson how to tell whether a child is gifted, and what to do if the answer is yes.

Mrs. Anderson says that finding out what people are good at is more important than looking at numbers, and it's not that important to try to tell the difference between kids who are gifted and ones who are just plain smart. What does matter is HOW the person thinks, and whether the person LIKES to think.

She was interested when my mom told her I liked to know how things work, and when she heard what I had done on that arithmetic paper, she said "people who are gifted usually like to play around with patterns, and they figure things out in original ways. Kids who are only precocious may enjoy memorizing better than thinking." She asked my mom to bring me over.

The first time I stayed more than an hour but it felt like a couple of minutes. First Mrs. Anderson showed me how to do math with some blocks and rods and shapes. Then she gave me some math puzzles to solve. They were hard but I liked them. I figured four different ways to do the last one, and she called me "a real live number-thinker." The way she said it made me feel proud.

Then we played word games; rhymes, opposites, riddles, and something called analogies. She said "feathers are light; rocks are... ?" and "thirsty goes with water the way hungry goes with... ?" She gave me words and asked me to tell what they meant, she asked me what was the same and what was different about two things; a bus and a boat, and then she'd name a category and I had to say all the words I could think of as fast as I could. I had so many my tongue could hardly keep up with my head. We both ended up laughing.

*T*hen Mrs. Anderson asked what she calls Explorer Questions; "what if it stayed light all the time and never ever ever got dark," and "what could you do if you wanted to weigh a giraffe?" She kept saying things like "I can tell you like new ideas" and " I can tell you like to puzzle things out." At the end, she gave me some designs to copy and she asked me to draw a house, a tree, and a person.

*O*n my second visit, she gave me some tests with words, numbers, blocks, pictures, and some shapes I had to copy in a hurry. After we were through, she and my mom and dad talked for a long time. They let me be there. "After all" Mrs. Anderson said, "we're talking about the way Evan thinks, Evan should be thinking about it with us."

Mrs. Anderson said she had measured my IQ on the second visit, and that my numbers would qualify for lots of programs for gifted kids. But she didn't think my score was as important as what she could tell about *the way* I think. She said that gifted people... not just kids... often think in special ways:

They seem to understand things right away without lots of explaining.

They notice patterns and play with them.

They have a lot of curiosity, they put energy into their ideas, they like to work on hard problems, and they can concentrate for long periods.

They often know how other people are feeling.

They notice things that other people overlook.

They have original ideas and sometimes they'd rather play with questions than just get correct answers.

*M*y mom and dad kept nodding and saying "Evan's like that." Mrs. Anderson agreed. I was glad because I thought so too.

Then she said that being what people call gifted (or just plain smart), isn't easy. Other kids, and grown-ups too, sometimes feel jealous or afraid. Mrs. Anderson said that gifted or smart kids need special help. The people taking care of them need to remember that first of all they are kids. After that, they are kids who learn in a special way. I felt really good when she talked about that.

She said gifted kids need to know that they belong... in their families, in school, and other places too. They know they are different because of the way they think, so they need extra help to feel connected to the rest of the world. Mrs. Anderson said that smart kids don't need to skip grades. There are lots of ways for parents, and teachers too, to let the kid stay with other kids the same age, and still make room for them to think in their own way.

*S*ometimes smart kids need help learning how to make friends. Taking care of a pet can help with the loneliness. Sometimes it's easier to be friends with someone older or younger, or a pet, than with kids in the same class.

She said kids who are learning new things, and playing with patterns, need outlets for their ideas so they don't explode.

Mrs. Anderson said we need to have a lot of true information to use in making up our new ideas, but we shouldn't just memorize facts; we shouldn't have to stick to what other people have already found out. We need to use our imaginations in music or art or acting. We need to use our bodies to explain some of our ideas and feelings. And we need chances to think about what's right and what's wrong. Some ideas could help other people or the world, other ones might hurt.

*S*he said we need grown-ups who think it's OK to take a chance on a new idea. Sometimes that happens in school, but when it doesn't, parents can compensate by showing that the world doesn't end over a mistake or two.

And then she said we need chances to laugh. Sometimes people expect smart kids to act grown-up all the time.

My dad said "But what about lessons and teaching. Does Evan need special teachers?"

"Yes," said Mrs. Anderson "teachers who are special in the way they love children, who know how to help them, and when to let them go on their own."

"But what about special training and degrees? Can regular parents and teachers do the job?" asked my mom.

"There's a professor out in Indiana named Dr. Bloom... I like that name, it's like a flower" said Mrs. Anderson. "He has studied what helps talents grow; warmth, encouragement, humor, and the parent's interest. Later on it's important to have special teachers, but in the beginning the most important thing is someone the child likes and who understands kids."

*M*rs. Anderson continued, "If we knew Evan would have perfect teachers every year, we could turn everything over to the school system, but things don't work that way. We need to plan so he'll be OK even when he doesn't have a perfect teacher. What ideas can we all come up with?

"I could check the library and the Saturday programs at the nearby college," said my mom. "I remember seeing one announcement about soccer, and another about learning to be a junior magician."

My dad said, "Or I could get together with some friends and have a Saturday morning club for others who are interested in what Evan likes to do, figuring out how to make things work."

"What ideas do you have Evan?" asked Mrs. Anderson.

"Well, I like what you said about teachers. I'd like to learn to read music if the teacher would also let me play the piano by ear. And I'd really like to have a dog to play with when I get home from school, and to sleep in my room at night. It would be great if there were some other kids to make things with on Saturday mornings, but I don't want to be on a schedule all weekend. I want time to play with my dog (if I get one) and there's stuff I like to read, and I want to be able to hang out, specially if I make some new friends who like to do what I like. There are two kids in my class who might join."

"I'd like both of us to talk to Evan's teacher" my dad said to my mom. "If we explain how Evan feels about the workbooks and worksheets, and the new things he's starting, maybe she'll make his paper work the same as everybody else's."

"Perhaps she was just trying to offer a challenge," Mrs. Anderson said. "Sometimes teachers aren't sure how to handle their quickest students. They give them more to do because they think that's a favor. If you like, I'll be glad to have a conference with her at school, in her classroom. I've been a teacher so maybe I can help. I can also suggest some things for her to read."

"I'd like to read more, too" said my dad. "The more we know the more we can work with Evan's teachers every year."

"If I have my Saturday projects, and time to hack around, and I can learn new music, and play with my dog, I guess I can stand the workbooks" I said. "And if some of the projects work out, maybe I can bring them to school so other kids can see how to do them too."

"**W**hy don't schools have programs for kids like Evan?" my mom asked.

"Some do" said Mrs. Anderson "But when money dries up so do the programs. And sometimes there are too many kids to fit in, so some who would do very well get left out and feel bad. Sometimes the program is only an hour a week, and sometimes it means the kids are taken out of class for a whole day, or one week out of four. Sometimes they are separated for a whole year or more. Some programs are perfect, others are hurtful. And lots of schools can't afford them. When the perfect program isn't available, parents have to fill in, with the help of the kid. It's wonderful when the teacher helps too."

Well, that all
happened a couple of months ago. My teacher
told my mom and dad she would cut my
paper work back, and that she had liked
talking to Mrs. Anderson. She said she had
been worried about me too, but she didn't
know what to do. I never knew TEACHERS
worried! She said she had given me extra
stuff so I wouldn't be bored. Now she lets me
read my library book if I'm the first to finish
my worksheets, and she set up a project
corner with some good weaving and art
things. A bunch of us are doing a class
newspaper, and she's made extra time for us
to work on it.

My mom and dad
signed me up for something called Explorers
Unlimited at the Y on Saturdays. We learn
how to make things, and my dad is going to
be one of the teachers. Two other kids from
my class go, and we eat pizza afterwards. I
don't feel like "the only one in the world" any
more.

My piano lessons are on Wednesdays and I can walk there by myself. My teacher is really nice! Part of the time she teaches me how to read notes and keep time. The other part she plays something for me, I watch and listen, and then I try to play it back to her. She always says "Evan, you're a natural!" Sometimes I sing when I play, and I'm getting much better.

I named my dog "Andy" after Mrs. Anderson. When I told her she said "Thanks! You can call me Andy too if you like, just as long as you don't expect me to wag my tail." That's what she's like. She likes to laugh.

Signs and Signals

Traits which often cluster together in gifted people:

Recognition of new material.

Awareness of patterns.

Drive, curiosity, energy, powerful concentration, empathy.

Strong memory for experiences and feeling, sometimes trouble memorizing.

Heightened perceptions.

Divergent thinking.

# of Gifted Thinking

Gifted people of all ages need:

A sense of belonging.

To give as well as receive care and attention.

A chance for output as well as intake of ideas.

Rational/scientific education, aesthetic nourishment, opportunities to explore ethical issues.

Adult leadership.

Humor.

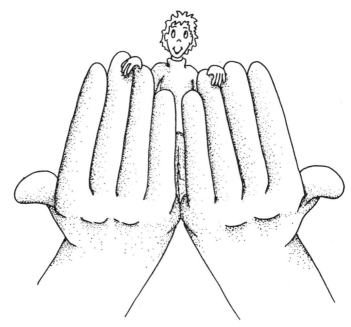

RESOURCE LIST
Books

Ames, Louise Bates. *What Do They Mean I'm Difficult?* Rosemont, New Jersey: Programs for Education, 1986.

Erikson, Erik H. *Childhood and Society.* New York: W.W. Norton, Inc. (revised), 1963.

Featherstone, Helen. *A Difference in the Family.* New York: Basic Books, 1980.

Healy, Jane M. *Your Child's Growing Mind.* New York: Doubleday, 1987.

Vail, Priscilla L. *Smart Kids With School Problems; Things to Know and Ways to Help.* New York: E.P. Dutton, due in September, 1987.

Vail, Priscilla L. *The World of the Gifted Child.* New York: Walker & Co., 1979.

Audio Tape

Vail, Priscilla L. *Raising Smart Kids; Commonsense, Uncommon Needs.* Programs for Education, Rosemont, New Jersey.

Priscilla L. Vail is a learning specialist at the Rippowam-Cisqua School in Bedford, NY and a mother of four.

In her work she gives special attention to educational alternatives now available for an atypical learner; the gifted, the learning disabled, and gifted students with Specific Language Disability.

A member of the American Association for Gifted Children and the World Council for Gifted and Talented, Ms. Vail is a nationally recognized authority on Learning Disabilities. She lectures and writes for such organizations as the Orton Dyslexia Society, National Association of Independent Schools, Bank Street College of Education and The Center for School Success.

She is on the Advisory Board of the Fisher-Landau Foundation, engaged in the development of programs for the gifted, learning disabled.

Other books by Priscilla Vail available from
Modern Learning Press/Programs for Education

Common Ground

About Dyslexia

Clear and Lively Writing

Smart Kids with School Problems

For more information, contact
Modern Learning Press/Programs for Education
P.O. Box 167
Rosemont, NJ 08556

or call toll-free
1-800-627-5867